The Seven V's of A Great Ea

Also in this series

The Seven C's of Positive Behaviour Management
The Seven E's of Reading for Pleasure
The Seven M's of Writing for a Living
The Seven P's of Brilliant Voice Usage
The Seven R's of Great Group Work
The Seven S's of Developing Young Writers
The Seven T's of Practical Differentiation

Also by Sue Cowley

Bad Faerie and the Grotto of the Goblins
The Calm Classroom: 50 Key Techniques for Better Behaviour
The Creative Classroom: 50 Key Techniques for Imaginative Teaching and Learning
How to Survive your First Year in Teaching, *third edition*
Getting the Buggers to Behave, *fifth edition*
Getting the Buggers into Drama
Getting the Buggers to Write, *third edition*
Getting the Buggers to Think, *second edition*
Guerilla Guide to Teaching, *second edition*
Sue Cowley's A-Z of Teaching
Sue Cowley's Teaching Clinic
Letting the Buggers be Creative
Getting your Little Darlings to Behave
The Road to Writing: A Step-By-Step Guide to Mark Making: 3-7
Teaching Skills for Dummies

The Seven V's of
A Great Early Years Setting

SUE COWLEY

Sue Cowley Books Ltd

2015

Sue Cowley Books Ltd
PO Box 1172
Bristol BS39 4ZJ

www.suecowley.co.uk

© **Sue Cowley Books Ltd**

First published 2015

Part of the 'Alphabet Sevens' Series

Also in this series:

The Seven C's of Positive Behaviour Management
The Seven E's of Reading for Pleasure
The Seven M's of Writing for a Living
The Seven P's of Brilliant Voice Usage
The Seven R's of Great Group Work
The Seven S's of Developing Young Writers
The Seven T's of Practical Differentiation

All rights reserved. No part of this publication may be reproduced or transmitted in any form or by any means, electronic or mechanical, including photocopying, recording, or any information storage or retrieval system, without prior permission in writing from the publishers.

Sue Cowley has asserted her right under the Copyright, Designs and Patents Act, 1988, to be identified as Author of this work.

ISBN: 978-1514301920

Contents

Introduction 1

The First V: Vision 3
   Identifying your Vision 5
   A 'Mission Statement' 8
   Sharing your Vision 9
   Reflecting on your Vision 11
   A Vision for Play 12

The Second V: Voice 13
   A Voice for the Children 15
   Safeguarding and Children's Voice 17
   A Voice for Parents 18
   A Voice for Staff 21
   A Voice for the Setting 23

The Third V: Verbal Communication 27
   The Power of Verbal Communication 28
   Great Verbal Communication 29
   Building Communication Skills 31
   Sustained Shared Thinking 33
   Sustained Shared Thinking in Action 35
   Supporting Children with Communication Difficulties 37

The Fourth V: Visual & Non-Verbal Communication 39
   Visual Communication 40
   Non-Verbal Communication 42
   Alternative Methods of Communication 43

The Fifth V: Variety 45
   A Variety of Skills and Subjects 46
   A Variety of Resources 47
   Finding Great Resources 48
   Managing Resources 50
   Creating your own Resources 51

A Variety of Environments/Experiences   52
The Setting Environment   53
Variety in the Outdoor Environment   55
A Variety of Approaches   56
Variety: Valuing Diversity   58
The Sixth V: Visits, Visitors and Volunteers   59
Trips and Visits   60
Visits and Transition   61
Visitors   62
Volunteers   63
The Seventh V: Viability   65
Financial Management   66
Marketing   69
Fundraising   70

Introduction

This book offers a concise and practical guide to developing and maintaining a high quality early years setting. As with all of my *Alphabet Sevens* guides, it is designed to be quick and easy to read, with plenty of realistic ideas that you can put into place straight away. In this guide I give lots of questions for you to ask yourselves in your setting, as part of an ongoing process of self-reflection and self-evaluation. Whether you work in a nursery, a preschool, a children's centre, a school nursery, or a reception class, this short guide is for you. Many of the elements in this guide will also be useful to you if you work as a nanny or a childminder. This book will help you develop a high quality setting, so that your children learn and develop in the best possible way while they are in your care.

Having trained as an early years/primary teacher, and after teaching in a variety of settings, I now work as a teacher trainer and education author. I have also helped to run my local preschool for the past six years. During this time I have learned a lot about how to make an early years setting as great as it can be. The aim of this book is to pass on the practical ideas I have discovered to other early years practitioners.

The early years sector is diverse, constantly changing and evolving: it runs from birth to the age of five. Increasingly, most young children attend some kind of early years setting in the time before they begin their statutory education, especially since the introduction of state funding for childcare. In some areas of the country, there is lots of early years provision within children's centres, and in nursery classes in state-run infant or primary schools. In other areas, there is little or no state-run provision before statutory school starting age, and instead there is a patchwork of privately run and voluntary run settings. As diverse as the sector is, I have found it to be characterised by committed practitioners and teachers, doing the very best for the children in their care.

The ideas in this book will help you step back and take an overview of the provision you offer to your children and their parents. This guide will help you identify those areas where you are already strong, and focus on those areas where you need to boost your provision. My mini guide will help you make your early years setting as 'great' as it can possibly be. This is not a guide about how to get an 'outstanding' inspection result, although the ideas here should help you be successful when the inspectors visit. Rather, this guide aims to help you create the very best provision for all your children. And I sincerely hope it helps you achieve just that.

Sue Cowley
www.suecowley.co.uk

Please note that I have used the term 'parents' in this book to describe whoever looks after the child. This could include foster parents, adoptive parents, looked after children, children cared for by siblings or other family members, and so on.

The First V:

Vision

The First V: Vision

Every education setting needs a vision of the care and education it aims to provide for its children: a clear understanding of the set of values that underpin everything that you do. This is sometimes referred to as an 'ethos'. An ethos underlies everything that goes on in your setting, and it is passed on to the children through everything that you do. A 'vision' is like having an invisible banner, pinned up over your door, which says: *'This is how we do it here.'* The clearer you are about your vision and values, and the better these aspects are understood by staff, children and parents, the more effective your setting will be. Where all the people who use or work in a setting buy into a consistent ethos, this is a very powerful force for learning and improvement.

Having a vision is about much more than just having a 'mission statement' that you put on your nursery banner, your preschool website, or your infant or primary school sign. It is about having a crystal clear view of what you want your early years setting to look, feel and be like for the children and families who use it. It is about having an ethos that runs through everything you do, like the message inside a stick of seaside rock. Sometimes a specific approach or theory about learning in the early years will underpin a setting's vision. For instance, a Montessori nursery will apply the principles set out by the early years educator Maria Montessori; a Forest School setting will place a strong emphasis on time spent outdoors. A clear and confidently expressed vision will help your setting be the best that it can be for all your children.

Identifying your Vision

The values that you have filter through into everything you do, particularly when all the staff share the same vision about what their early years setting should be like. It is far better to develop an ethos that is shared by all staff, rather than to try to impose one person's vision on the rest of a staff team. Here are some key questions to help you identify what your vision is:

- ✓ What is your vision of the role of play in the early years? This may seem like an obvious question, but there are various different ideas about the kind of play that early years settings should encourage and develop. There is an emphasis at the moment on 'purposeful play', but we should take care that this does not translate into a vision of play where the adults have high levels of control. At its heart, play must be led by the children; it should involve them having agency in their own learning.
- ✓ How will you ensure that the children feel in control of their learning, and help them stay fully engaged throughout their time in your setting? How will you handle any issues with difficult behaviour, or with children who struggle to settle?
- ✓ What is your local area like and how will this impact on what you do in your setting? How will you use the area around your setting as part of what you offer the children, for instance using local green spaces or offering cultural opportunities? Think about places you can visit and use as part of what you offer, but also consider what may be *missing* in terms of the early experiences that your children have had. For instance, in a rural setting with little diversity, you might place a priority on ensuring the children get to experience a wide range of cultures. In an

urban setting, your focus might be on gaining experience of nature and the outside world.
- ✓ What do those families who use your setting want from your setting, and how can you involve them as closely as possible in their children's development and learning? How will you go about building partnerships with the families who use your provision, and supporting the children's learning and development when they are at home?
- ✓ What aspects of safety, health and welfare does your setting prioritise? Clearly, these are important for all children, but your focus might vary according to your children's needs. For instance, if oral hygiene is a key issue in your area, how can you offer families plenty of support?
- ✓ How will you ensure that your setting is welcoming and inclusive to all? Does your setting feel accessible to all those families who might benefit from it? If there are many different languages in the local area, or a range of cultures, how will you overcome any barriers to access?
- ✓ What is your vision around supporting children with special educational needs or disabilities? How will you ensure they gain all the support that is available to them? Is your setting physically accessible to all children who have a disability? Do you use Makaton or British Sign Language, to support children with communication difficulties?
- ✓ What role do you want the outdoors and the natural world to play in your setting? Can the children move freely between indoors and outdoors when they are with you? Is your focus perhaps going to be on growing fruit and vegetables, spending lots of time in the outdoors, or perhaps even keeping some animals?

- ✓ How do you feel that an early years setting can help children to become confident and happy learners? How can you help preschool aged children get ready to move on to school? In a reception class, how will you help your children prepare for the more formal environment of key stage one?
- ✓ What kind of environment do you aspire to create? How will you ensure that the environment feels comfortable and welcoming to everyone who comes there? If your setting has particular safety issues (for instance, if it is near a busy road), how will you ensure that the children are secure as they travel to your setting, and when they are with you? What role do aspects such as lighting, resources and equipment play in your vision of a welcoming environment for the children?
- ✓ How do you work with local schools, to ensure a smooth transition for the children in your care? If your children move on to a number of different primary schools, how will you manage the administrative difficulties of maintaining contact? What kind of information do you pass on to primary schools, and how do you do this, so that teachers are well informed about the needs of the children who join them? How can you encourage teachers from local primary schools to visit your setting, as well as the children visiting them in preparation for transition?
- ✓ What kind of opening hours does your setting have or aspire to achieve, and for which ages of children? Our preschool is a part time setting, offering a place for local children to play and socialise for a few hours each day. A full daycare setting might place a focus on supporting parents who need to go to work, caring for babies as well as young children.

A useful exercise is to ask each staff member at your setting to make a list of words that describe the vision and values they want to achieve. Look together at the words your staff members have listed, asking each person to talk about why she or he chose those particular words. Do some words come up several times? Does your setting struggle to achieve any of these stated values, and why is this? Are there three words that everyone agrees on?

A 'Mission Statement'

A tagline or 'mission statement' for your setting gives staff, parents and children a sense of 'what you are about'. This statement also reminds you of the overall direction in which you want to go. Your statement should sum up what your vision is. It is tricky to develop a mission statement, because you probably have lots of different aspects that you would like to incorporate. You might find it useful to think about what your focus is in relation to the following areas:

- ✓ How you want the children to learn while they are in your setting – which approaches do you believe work best for your children?
- ✓ How do you want the children to feel when they are with you, including those who are new to your setting?
- ✓ How do you want parents to feel about using your setting, and about leaving their children in your care?
- ✓ How will you work together with parents, to help them support their children's learning and development at home, as well as in your setting?
- ✓ What kind of skills, attitudes and attributes do you want the children to develop? How do you want them to see themselves as learners?

Our setting uses the tagline: *"Happy children; Confident learners"*. We felt this summed up our vision, which is about engagement, self-confidence and building independence. We wanted it to be clear that we put the children's emotional well being first, with a focus on children feeling happy in their learning while they are with us.

Sharing your Vision

It is often the case that the setting leader and the people who manage the setting have a clear sense of vision for the setting. However, it can be hard to get other people on board. Consider how you can help your children, staff, parents and others to understand your vision and values as well. To do this:

- ✓ Model your vision in every single interaction you have with your children. Your children will sense it if you mean what you say, through the way that you interact with them each day.
- ✓ Ensure that parents get a say in the kind of vision that you have: an early years setting does not operate in a vacuum, it is *for* the children and their parents. One useful way to do this is to ask parents to write you a short letter about their child, when he or she first starts at your setting. What does the child especially enjoy? What fears or worries does the child have? What do the parents want for their child while he or she is with you? Is there anything about the child's background that it would be useful for staff to know?
- ✓ Use training, supervisory meetings and staff appraisals to ensure that staff members understand your vision, and to help them develop the right skills to create and sustain it. Set clear targets, so that your staff members know the

areas in which they need to improve or develop. Offer high quality training so that staff can develop areas of interest, and gain support in aspects of their practice where they are not so strong. Have plenty of staff meetings where you talk about how you are progressing towards the vision you have expressed. A daily 'staff briefing' is very useful, both to talk about day-to-day issues, and also to reinforce your vision.

- ✓ When you employ new staff, look for those who have a clear vision of what early years education should look like, one that chimes with your setting's vision. Talk to them about their views on areas such as early learning and development, the role of the practitioner, building relationships with parents, and on the importance of play in early learning.
- ✓ Share examples of good practice with other settings and across the sector. For instance, you might arrange a networking event, where practitioners from other settings visit to see the approaches you use, and share what they do with you as well. You can also use Twitter and Facebook to exchange ideas and information.

Share your 'mission statement' widely, so that everyone is clear about your vision. For instance, your statement could appear:

- ✓ On the walls of your setting;
- ✓ In any advertising that you do;
- ✓ In correspondence with parents;
- ✓ In your prospectus;
- ✓ On your website, emails and on any social media that your setting uses;
- ✓ On your banner and any signs outside your setting.

Reflecting on your Vision

The best early years settings do not stand still, or rest on their laurels, even if they receive an 'Outstanding' report from Ofsted, or if all the parents and children seem to love what they do. A great early years setting will be involved in a constant process of improvement, and the best way to do this is through reflection and self-evaluation. The way that parents feel about your setting is a great test of how well you are doing. Parents sense if their children are unsettled or uncomfortable, so make it easy for them to share any concerns.

The very best way for your setting to move forwards, and to improve, is through using an on-going process of self-evaluation. Self-evaluation is not simply about completing an Ofsted 'self-evaluation form', or taking part in a system of quality assurance. Self-evaluation should never be about jumping through the right hoops to get a good inspection result. For self-evaluation to be effective, you must:

- ✓ Know where your setting is at the moment, in all aspects of your provision;
- ✓ Work out, as a whole staff team, what needs to be done to take it forwards;
- ✓ Figure out a plan and a timescale in which to do those things;
- ✓ Ensure that the relevant actions are completed at the expected time;
- ✓ Start over again at the beginning, so that your setting constantly improves.

Having experimented with the Ofsted format, our setting has now adopted a self-evaluation framework called The Bristol Standard instead. We felt that this framework supported us in an in depth, ongoing and high quality process of self-evaluation. Experiment until you find the self-evaluation approach that works best for you. Make sure that this does not become a paperwork exercise that is done once, then filed away and forgotten until it needs an update.

A Vision for Play

We might feel it is fairly straightforward to articulate our vision for play, but a quick look at the visions of different organisations on the subject is very instructive. The term 'purposeful play' is increasingly being used, particularly in communications from Ofsted, suggesting that a specific type of play is most valuable. As a staff team, talk together about what play means to you, and in your setting:

- ✓ To what extent do the children have free choice of how, when, where and what to play while they are at your setting?
- ✓ To what extent is children's play in your setting 'directed' by adults?
- ✓ How do you decide when to join in with children's play, and when to step back and observe it?
- ✓ Who does most of the talking during play in your setting – the children or the adults?
- ✓ How do you use 'observations' and 'next steps', to decide what resources or experiences to offer? How do you react if the children decide not to take the 'next steps' that you suggest for them?
- ✓ How do different staff members define 'play' – what input would they expect the adult to have when the children are playing?
- ✓ How far do you believe play can be 'taught', and how far do you see it as a natural, instinctive activity for children?

The Second V:

Voice

The Second V: Voice

Listening is a critical skill for anyone who works in education. If we fail to listen to others, we miss out on many great opportunities for thinking, improving, developing and learning. We can listen to ideas for activities from our colleagues; we can listen to parents when they tell us that their child enjoys a particular kind of activity. We can listen to the children's ideas about where or how they would like to play; we can listen to advice from others on how best to improve our settings. Of course, each and every day, we listen to our children to find out what they need or want to learn, what they might need from us to do this, what kind of activities they would like to do, what they feel, and what they are thinking about.

Ideally, both the parent's and the child's voices should be heard and listened to throughout a child's education. There should also be the feeling that the educational setting responds to what is being said, as appropriate. This is especially important in the early years, because young children cannot always communicate their wishes and feelings fully. This is not to say that settings should do exactly what parents tell them to do. However, when you make a professional judgement about how to run your provision, you should be prepared to explain your reasoning to your parents.

For instance, in the past we have had parents who requested that we do more 'tracing over names' activities with their children to help them learn to write. We looked at these requests and felt that parents needed to know more about early language acquisition. So, in response we sent out a short leaflet, ran a parent workshop, and put more information in our newsletter. Communication is a two way process. The best early years environments give everyone a chance to have their say and to make a contribution to the success of the setting. Babies and the smallest children may not be able to contribute verbally. However, we can read the cues and clues they give us – a smile or gurgle, pushing a toy away – and 'hear' their voices loud and clear.

A Voice for the Children

There are many ways you can ensure that your children's voices are heard, both within your day-to-day provision, and also in the longer-term vision that you have for your setting. Here are some strategies that work well:

- ✓ **Children's play:** One of the best ways to 'hear' what a young child is 'saying', is to watch him or her at play. Children speak very loudly through their play – we can see what their interests are, what they already know, what kind of skills they need to develop, and so on. Take time to observe children at play in your setting, taking note of the next steps that are required, or the topics that interest them.
- ✓ **Children's choice:** When you plan activities and resources for your setting each day, leave at least one area free, so that the children can decide what they would like to do there. If you have an accessible cupboard or other storage space, you might ask a few children to look at the resources and decide what they would like to play with.
- ✓ **Visual choices:** Make a book with photographs of all the different resources on offer in your setting (this could be done as a slideshow on a tablet instead). Show the book to your children, either first thing in the morning or the previous day, and ask them what *they*

would like to play with. This technique is especially useful for pack-away settings and for childminders, where there are often lots of resources available, but it is not possible to have them all accessible at once. A 'choices board' also works well: the children are shown photos of resources, and they stick the ones they would like to play with on the board.

- ✓ **Accessing resources:** If you have permanent space for lots of resources, consider how the children will know what is where. Label drawers with a picture or photo of what is inside. Dedicate different spaces to different types of resources, for instance with an area for literacy and another for numeracy. Take care that there is not too much choice, as that can make it hard for children to focus or choose. The children are also prone to mix up all your resources, leaving you with a big tidying job.
- ✓ **Planning boards:** If you have a limited space, for instance in a small reception classroom, use planning boards to help the children spread out between the different areas or activities. Create a board for each area (e.g. role play, construction, water play, small world, etc.) and then add a number of Velcro squares. The children stick their names (or photos) up on the board of their choice. When all the squares are full, this means that the activity is full and they must choose something else for the time being. Get the children to swap activities after an agreed period of time.
- ✓ **Show and tell:** This format is great for helping young children to build confidence in speaking, and focus in listening. Ask the children to bring in a familiar object daily, which they place in the show and tell box on arrival. Whenever there is time during the day, encourage them to talk about the toy or object they brought in.

What is it, why did they choose to bring it in, and does anyone have any questions about it? Depending on the children's confidence, they might do this individually with a practitioner, with a small group of friends, or in a large group format.
- ✓ **Just talk:** When you play with the children, or update their learning journeys, talk together about what they like to do, what they feel about different aspects of your setting, and so on. It is also useful to do a short 'exit interview' or questionnaire for parents and children when they move on to school, or into a new key stage, to find out how they felt about being in your setting.
- ✓ **Observations:** Babies and young children cannot necessarily express what they mean. We need to learn to look closely and to 'listen' to the way that they play. We should consider what the choices they make 'say' about them and how they are feeling, and also consider what their non-verbal signals and gestures mean. As you observe children at play, consider what they are telling you about their interests, needs, fascinations, and so on.

Safeguarding and Children's Voice

Safeguarding is a key role for early years practitioners – it is everyone's responsibility. Young children are often not in a position to make their situation known, and so all practitioners must be alert to signs of abuse or neglect. Ensure that:

- ✓ Your setting has a designated professional lead for safeguarding – usually the setting leader. In a school setting, this may well be the head teacher.
- ✓ Staff are fully trained in child protection, and understand how to spot and report concerns, as quickly as possible.

- ✓ All adults working with the children have passed the relevant checks, and obtained full clearance. In a voluntary run setting, all committee members must have a DBS check and suitability letter from Ofsted. The Chair of the committee should also have an Ofsted 'suitable person' interview.
- ✓ All adults are clear about the process for referrals, with all staff understanding the role of your Local Safeguarding Children Board and local authority social care team. All staff understand how to share their concerns with other professionals.
- ✓ You put the needs and views of children first at all times, rather than those of adults. If you notice that a child seems troubled, or there are signs of neglect, you must act on your worries.
- ✓ Assess and monitor children at risk of neglect, monitor and record the impact of any services delivered to the child and family, regularly reviewing the help being given. Focus on the outcomes achieved for the child, and understand that intervention is an ongoing process, and not a single event.

A Voice for Parents

Find as many ways as possible for your parents' voices to be heard. Parents are your clients (along with their children), and it is only right that they give their input and opinions about the service you provide. This is not to say that you do exactly what the parents want you to, especially if you know that their requests are not what is best for the children. But remember that parents are their child's first and most enduring carers. They know their child as a unique individual. Teachers and practitioners miss a trick if they do not talk with parents about their feelings, opinions and ideas. It can sometimes prove tricky to ensure that parents' voices are heard, for instance this can be a problem if:

- ✓ Someone other than the parents picks up the children.
- ✓ Parents are working full time, and struggle to respond to requests for information.
- ✓ There are language barriers, or other communication difficulties, that make it hard for parents to communicate.
- ✓ Parents do not seem interested in letting you know what they think, or do not appear to have the confidence to do so.

Where there are issues such as those listed above, think creatively about how you can simplify the process of listening. The simpler and easier it is to communicate, the more likely your parents are to do it. Consider visual methods or try offering questionnaires in different community languages. At our setting we use a variety of methods to hear parent voice, and we analyse these approaches to see how effective they are (for instance, counting how many questionnaire responses we receive). To help parents communicate their opinions, try the following strategies:

- ✓ **Home visits:** A home visit is a great way to communicate with parents, and it is a great idea to offer a visit to all those who attend your setting. A visit to the child's home can help you understand much more about the child and his or her parents. You can get a feel for all the positive aspects of the child's home, as well as noting any issues that mean you might need to support the child in a specific way.

- ✓ **Informal chats:** In many ways, the best time to hear the parents' voices is when they drop their children off at your setting. If you have a defined time for drop off, a practitioner can stand at the door to register children, find out who will do the pick up, and have a quick chat to parents. It can be tempting to want to get the children in quickly, and the parents away quickly as well, so that you can 'get on with' your day. However, this time is a great opportunity for communication between the setting and the families who use it.
- ✓ **Meetings:** You can talk in slightly more depth at a parents' meeting to report on progress. Make sure to ask the question: 'is there anything you want to ask/share with us?' Some parents may be nervous to raise any issues, so make it clear that you value their feedback.
- ✓ **A comments book:** Leave a small comments book somewhere obvious – we keep ours just above the children's drawers, so that it is available when parents help to change reading books. Remind parents regularly to leave their thoughts or comments – otherwise they tend to forget. Stick any 'thank you' cards that are given to the setting into your comments book as well.
- ✓ **Questionnaires:** It's tempting to send out long questionnaires, in the hope of gathering lots of opinions and information. Balance the desire to find out what people are thinking with the benefit of actually getting questionnaires returned. Keep your questionnaires brief, so that the majority of parents respond. We use a short series of 'tickbox' style questions, with a space for more detailed responses. In our setting we send out two questionnaires: one to all parents at Easter time, then a second one to the parents of those children who are

leaving to go to school, towards the end of the Summer term.
- ✓ **A comments thread on your blog:** At our setting we post a weekly blog, which gives information about what the children have been doing in sessions during the week. Parents love our blog because they can find out exactly what their children have been doing that week, and talk about it with them at home. They can also leave comments on the blog to communicate with the setting or simply to thank staff or leave a positive comment.
- ✓ **Learning Journeys/EYFS profiles:** Parents love the learning journeys and profiles that settings create for their children. It is lovely to see the progress your child has made, and to share all the exciting things that they are learning. Although updating these documents takes time, it is a great way for staff to learn more about their children and see how they are progressing. These documents are also brilliant for transition, as they give the next teacher/practitioner a sense of where the child is now. You can use digital learning journeys (such as Tapestry – see www.eyfs.info) that allow parents to add comments as well.
- ✓ **Key workers:** Parents really value having one person as their main point of contact. The key worker system is brilliant for achieving this – when parents and children know who their key worker is, they can go straight to that person if they have any questions, queries or concerns.

A Voice for Staff

If staff members communicate well together, this ensures that your setting runs at its best. Where there are disagreements amongst staff, this can lead to tensions, which in turn impacts on how well staff are able to care for the children. Wherever possible, encourage staff to find the appropriate channels for voicing their opinions.

- ✓ **Regular staff meetings:** Depending on the number of staff you employ, you might timetable a weekly or fortnightly staff meeting. This regular meeting could be used to talk about planning, disseminate information from any training that staff members have attended, or to share information and ideas about the children.
- ✓ **Morning briefings:** It can work very well to have a short five-minute briefing at the start of each day, especially if all or most of your staff begin work at the same time. This briefing helps develop a sense of a staff team working together, and it is also useful for communicating short or urgent messages.
- ✓ **Suggestions box:** If your staff members are not overly confident about speaking out, an anonymous suggestions box is a great way for them to communicate with the setting and the manager. Encourage them to leave positive suggestions as well as negative ones, perhaps by having a small prize for any ideas that get used.
- ✓ **Appraisals:** Remember that appraisals are not just about the setting leader and manager/committee member talking to the staff member: they are also about staff communicating with the setting. Leave plenty of time for annual staff appraisals, to ensure that staff can talk about their hopes for the future, any training they might need or want to do, or other similar issues that they might not wish to raise at a full staff meeting. Use a termly supervisory meeting, to help staff keep on track with targets, and to allow staff to raise any issues or questions.

A Voice for the Setting

Your setting needs to find a way to make its voice heard as well. Sometimes the messages that you have to communicate will be for parents, about general administrative issues. At other times you will want to communicate with parents about their child's learning. Your setting should also communicate with the local community and with prospective new parents. You might want to communicate with local sources of support as well, such as charities offering grants for a voluntary run setting, or the early years team at your local authority.

For instance, if there are issues of safety around the area where your setting is based, get in touch with your local council. One of the issues that we had at our setting was that the journey was dangerous for those children walking to preschool. Our setting is in the centre of a village, with no pavements as you walk towards the building. We got in touch with the Transport team at our local authority, who sent a representative out to have a look at the issues. After our meeting, the council agreed to install a 'fake pavement' and some additional road signs, to create a safer route to preschool for parents and children.

When you communicate with parents, take care about the tone of voice that you use. Steer well clear of being patronising and try your very hardest not to sound like you are nagging (even when you are!). Be aware of the variety of languages that are spoken by the parents of children at your setting. Make sure that you offer materials in different community languages, as appropriate, to ensure that your setting voice is accessible to all. We have found that parents are understandably keen to know what their children do each day at our setting, and that we regularly need to communicate messages to parents. There are various ways to go about this:

- ✓ **A parent noticeboard:** We have experimented with different kinds of parent noticeboards, positioning them in various spots, both inside and outside the setting. We now have one waterproof noticeboard outside the setting, where our parents wait, and another near the children's trays inside. Remember: a noticeboard is only useful if parents actually read it. When you are a busy parent, dropping off your child for the day before you rush off to work or to care for a younger child, the last thing you want to do is read long lists of messages from the setting. If there is a place just outside your setting, where parents wait to come in or stop for a chat after dropping off their children, this is the perfect spot to put up notices.
- ✓ **A learning noticeboard**: Our parents told us that they wanted to know more about the activities that were going on in our setting, so we started using a 'What we're doing today' noticeboard. The board lists some of the activities that will be on offer; it also explains what the children will learn by doing these particular activities.
- ✓ **Newsletters:** A monthly or termly newsletter is a great way to pass on administrative messages and other key points to parents. Take care that the tone does not start to sound nagging (as in 'we have requested several times that parents label their children's clothes and some parents have still not done this'). Use your newsletter to give short messages and to highlight any positive events, such as fundraisers or trips.
- ✓ **Website:** It is vital these days to have a setting website. This might be a small, home-spun affair, like we have for

our voluntary run preschool where literally every penny counts. If your setting has a bigger budget, you might invest money in a professionally designed site. To create our website, we used the free website maker: www.weebly.com. We wanted our 'own' domain name so we purchased this for the setting and then 'pointed' the Weebly website to our new name. You can find instructions about how to do this at your hosting company, and at the Weebly site.

✓ **Blog:** We have found our weekly blog is a fantastic way for the setting to communicate with parents. It's also brilliant as a record for prospective new parents (and indeed, inspectors), so that they can see what the children have done each week. At first, we were concerned about whether parents would actually read our blog, but a recent questionnaire highlighted that it was one of our most popular methods of communication. Our staff pass on notes to our admin person about what they have been doing with the children. She then types up the blog entry and posts it on the same day each week.

✓ **Email and texts:** We use a weekly email to share the link to our blog, and we also include a 'Tip for Talk' idea in the email, for parents to use at home. Text messages are very useful for urgent communications between the setting and the home – for instance, they came in very handy when it snowed and staff could not get into work. When emailing parents, remember to keep email addresses private by using the 'blind copy' rather than the 'carbon copy' option.

✓ **Twitter and Facebook:** Many settings now use social media to communicate with parents, and the wider world, and to share news about the great things they are doing. Clearly, there is a time and personnel commitment in running any social media. Take care to think about issues of privacy, confidentiality, data protection and suitable content as well. Do not post any photos of children without the express permission of parents. At our setting we use photos of resources, artwork or activities rather than images of individual children.

- ✓ **Workshops:** Hosting a workshop is a great way to communicate information about different aspects of your provision, or to pass on great ideas for activities to support learning at home. Useful topics for workshops include early language development, behaviour management, and supporting reading at home. When offering a workshop, we have found it works well to combine a short Powerpoint presentation with some hands on activities and time for Q&A.
- ✓ **Leaflets and pamphlets:** Sometimes a short homemade leaflet or pamphlet is the best way to communicate specific information. For instance, a pamphlet to explain about how early years funding works, to give parents tips on supporting their children in early reading at home, or to give advice on dealing with nits. Your local authority or specialist support team may be able to provide you with leaflets to pass onto parents, rather than you having to create your own.
- ✓ **The press:** The local press are a great way to get your 'setting voice' out into the public arena. Local newspapers are typically very happy for you to send in a short report on a newsworthy event at your setting. They will often feature a photograph alongside the report, so make sure that you take photos and get parental permission as appropriate.

The Third V:

Verbal Communication

The Third V: Verbal Communication

At its heart, education is about communication: the early years practitioner or teacher communicates with the children, and in doing so, helps them to learn and develop. One of the secrets of success in the early years, and in all the years of education that follow, is to help staff learn to communicate brilliantly with their children. Those practitioners who communicate effectively will build strong and sensitive relationships with their children, and will help them to learn during their time in your early years setting.

On the face of it, communication seems like a simple act, about the natural process of speaking and listening. But while some people are brilliant communicators, others need support to communicate as effectively as possible. Fortunately, there are many techniques that practitioners can learn, in order to help them improve their communication skills. You can find lots of ideas about how to develop highly effective communication in this section.

The Power of Verbal Communication

Language development is critical to children's early learning and development, and high quality verbal communication is a must for a great early years setting. Although babies and very small children might not yet be able to communicate using words we would recognise, talk is as vital for them as it is for older children. The more that we listen to and talk with young children, the quicker their communication skills develop. It is quite astonishing really, how babbling quickly develops into coherent speech for the majority of young children. When we talk with children, this helps them to:

- ✓ Understand what we want, need or feel;
- ✓ Build a wide vocabulary;
- ✓ Pick out the sounds of different words;
- ✓ Learn how to listen, and how to focus on what someone is saying;
- ✓ Communicate their ideas, thoughts, feelings and opinions;
- ✓ Build confidence in expressing what they want/need/think;
- ✓ Gain knowledge of key concepts and facts;
- ✓ Build conceptual understanding;
- ✓ Develop an understanding of the internal grammar of language;
- ✓ Develop their social and emotional skills, and learn how to socialise with peers and adults;
- ✓ Learn to read people's emotional state, and build empathy;
- ✓ Understand more about the non-verbal aspects of communication, such as facial expression and gesture;
- ✓ Develop the phonological awareness that they need to learn how to read and write.

Great Verbal Communication

When we strive for great verbal communication, it is not just the amount of talk that we do that matters. The quality of the talk that we do has a huge impact on our children's learning and development – both what we say, and the way that we say it. It is also vital to make sure that children are listening when we speak to them – this might sound obvious, but some children really struggle to focus and maintain attention on what others are saying. Pause before you speak, to ensure you have the child's attention.

However, do remember that children on the autistic spectrum, and those from some cultures, sometimes prefer not to make direct eye contact when speaking to an adult. To achieve the highest quality talk possible, you should consider:

- ✓ **Tone of voice:** Children pick up a lot of cues and clues from the sound of our voices when we talk to them. With young children it is important to over emphasise your tone, so that you sound really happy, or really excited, curious, or interested. When we adapt our tone of voice, this also changes the way that we use our faces. Your eyes might widen or narrow, your eyebrows could lift or scrunch up. These clues are especially important for children who have English as an additional language. Think about how you work out what someone is saying when you travel overseas – you look at all the cues that they give, including gesture, facial expressions and body language, to try and gather meaning.
- ✓ **Type of voice:** It is tempting to use 'baby talk' when talking to young children – to use a very basic selection of words, a childlike voice, and overly simplified grammar. However, while it is important to use a clear voice, to slow down your pace, and to use reasonably simple vocabulary, it is not helpful for children's language development to completely change the way that you speak.
- ✓ **Choice of vocabulary:** The words that we use help our children both to understand what we are saying, and also to build a wider vocabulary. With very young children we need to use a simple vocabulary, but at the same time we should include words that will be new to the child, in different contexts. For instance, when talking about size,

you might note that something is "very small" and also "tiny" (but probably not "miniscule" just yet).
- ✓ **Emphasis:** We can help children to understand what we are saying by putting an emphasis on the key words within our speech. Create emphasis by using a slightly louder volume for key words, by adding a pause after you have said the word, or by slowing down what you are saying. For instance, when giving instructions, you can emphasise words that suggest time order, to help children understand sequencing ("first", "next", "finally").
- ✓ **Pace:** Avoid speaking too quickly when talking with young children, as they need to pick out the sense of what you are saying. While a fast pace is useful to motivate children to do something ("let's tidy away the toys" said enthusiastically), generally speaking you should speak slightly slower with children than you would with an adult.
- ✓ **The way we correct speech:** When children say a word incorrectly, it is tempting to correct them. However, this can tend to stunt communication rather than encourage it. The best approach is to repeat the word in context. So, if a child says "the block is lellow" you might say "yes, it is yellow", with an emphasis on the 'y' sound, rather than saying to the child "the correct word is 'yellow'".

Building Communication Skills

There are many ways that you can help your children to build their communication skills. Most children will talk and listen naturally during play, particularly when playing in a small group with other children or with adults. You can incorporate small group talking activities, and encourage speaking and listening as a whole class or large group, as well as more generally during your sessions. To build communication skills:

✓ Use lots of poems, nursery rhymes and songs in your setting, adding props to bring these to life. For instance, you could have some sausages sizzling in a pan as you sing the accompanying rhyme. When children move around the setting, this is a great time to incorporate singing, for instance doing counting songs as you walk to the seats at snack time.
✓ Talk about the routines you are using, as you use them, for instance talking to a baby about each step of what you are doing as you change his or her nappy.
✓ Show your children how to make different sounds, and help them work out which parts of our lips, teeth and tongues we use to say different letters or words. You can model this for them yourself, and you can also get the children to do this with a mirror, so that they can watch to see what happens to their faces.
✓ Offer lots of opportunities for speaking and listening in different contexts – both real and imaginary. This could include trips and visits, imaginary role play settings, and talk during show and tell sessions.
✓ Incorporate resources that encourage lots of speaking and listening – telephones, CDs, talk buttons, and so on.
✓ Ask questions to encourage your children to speak with you, and encourage them to ask questions of each other, by using question and answer type activities.
✓ Use self-talk and parallel talk when you are playing with your children. Self-talk is basically thinking out loud ("I'm wondering what we should do next"). Parallel talk

means narrating what the child is doing ("I can see that you have chosen the blue block to go on your tower next").
- ✓ Consider the noise levels in your setting, and create quiet times and spaces during the day. Encourage your children to listen and focus, as well as to talk and be noisy. Where possible, take them outside to listen to sounds in the natural world as well.
- ✓ When you talk to your children, give them plenty of time to respond. Make sure that they do not feel rushed to give answers or offer ideas.
- ✓ Be aware of the impact of environmental noise – living in a very noisy environment (for instance, near an airport or a busy road) can impact on children's learning and communication.

Sustained Shared Thinking

Sustained shared thinking is a wonderful way to help children learn to communicate their ideas, and to help them develop their thinking and understanding at the same time. With this technique, you use discussion, questions and the input of ideas as you play alongside your children, to help them to develop their thinking. Sustained shared thinking is:

- ✓ Sometimes initiated by the adult, but often initiated by the child – listen out for the clues and cues that tell you when it would be helpful to follow a child's chain of thought.
- ✓ About using a high percentage of open-ended questions, ones that encourage further questions, rather than lots of ones that ask for answers. Phrases such as "I wonder how …" and "I'm interested to know whether …" can help you do this.

- ✓ Often about playing with objects or materials together, exploring them and figuring out more about how they work or what they do.
- ✓ Helpful for the child's socio-dramatic development, for instance by constructing a shared imaginative world together, gradually adding to and building the imaginative context as you play.
- ✓ Extended by incorporating resources, asking questions, and suggesting other routes or possibilities for the child's exploratory thinking.
- ✓ Great for building collaborative and co-operative skills, and also for spontaneous wonder and curiosity.

Sustained shared thinking is a technique that practitioners can develop over time, through the process of working with, and listening to, the children. Aim to:

- ✓ Ask questions in a tone of wonder, as though you are talking to yourself, rather than specifically asking the child. This helps leave space for children to consider what you have said, rather than feeling that they must immediately give you an answer.
- ✓ Repeat and develop what the child has said, to extend his or her thinking. You might 'develop' an idea by rephrasing it using slightly more complex vocabulary, or by introducing a technical term (such as 'volume' in the example below).
- ✓ Ask questions that help the child move laterally from the thinking that has already been done. (Often the children will do this naturally, as well as with your input.)
- ✓ Be sensitive to learning opportunities, but try not to shoe horn them in, if the child does not choose to take the conversation laterally. Intervene in subtle ways,

following the child's train of thought. If the child chooses not to pick up on what you say, there is no need to push.
✓ Notice how a child substitutes a real object for a symbol – for instance, a wooden brick becomes a telephone, on which the child starts to have a pretend conversation. Taking on roles like this helps the child develop imaginative, symbolic thinking, so it is a very good way to extend thinking. Take on a role, yourself, within the child's play, for instance picking up a block of your own, to act as another telephone and to hold a pretend conversation.
✓ Listen really carefully to what your children are saying, to help you figure out what they are thinking, and to check for any misconceptions. This will help you know when it is appropriate to give answers, and when it would be better to ask further questions.
✓ Help children gradually build levels of abstract thinking, by showing them how concrete objects can be used to understand ever more abstract terms or concepts. Be sensitive about when to introduce new ideas and vocabulary, depending on the needs and the age of the child.
✓ You can also extend the child's thinking by giving them access to other resources – for instance, talking about a book you have in your setting that might give them an answer, or another toy that does something similar to the one you are playing with.

Sustained Shared Thinking in Action

Perhaps the best way to understand sustained shared thinking, is to see how it might work in practice. Here is an sample 'script', of an interaction between an early years practitioner and a child, showing how this technique can be used to develop thinking.

[The child is pouring water from one jug into another.]

Practitioner: *What are you doing, Amy?*

Amy: *I'm making a waterfall.*

Practitioner: *Ah, I see. How are you making it?*

Amy: *I'm pouring water from this, into this.* [Amy has two jugs: one is bigger than the other.] *I keep getting splashed though 'cos not all the water fits into this one!*

Practitioner: [giving a puzzled look and talking to herself] *Hmm ... I wonder why that is?*

Amy: *Because this one is bigger than this one.* [indicating the larger jug]

Practitioner: *Do you think it holds more water than the smaller one?* [Amy nods] *So it has a bigger volume. That means it holds more of something.*

Amy: *I saw a waterfall when I went for a walk by the river with my daddy. That waterfall splashed me too.*

Practitioner: *I wonder why it splashed you?*

Amy: *It was hitting a rock when it fell down, so maybe the water pushed it up.*

Consider what you might say next, and the kind of learning that Amy could get if you took this conversation in different directions.

Supporting Children with Communication Difficulties

While most children pick up language very quickly, some children will struggle with language development. Remember that children develop at different paces, and in different ways. For instance, some small children speak very little for a long time, and then suddenly start talking in full sentences. Be aware that a child who lacks confidence, or who is struggling to settle, may speak very little at first. If you teach a nursery or reception class, remember that your children may be up to a year apart in age.

Where a child appears to have a language delay, there are a number of potential causes to explore. Sometimes it is about an issue with hearing – for instance, children who have glue ear are likely to lag behind because they are not hearing as much speech, and find it difficult to hear the sounds that they themselves make. The problem might be to do with specific learning difficulties, or it might be about a lack of talk at home. Sometimes the issue is to do with a difficulty in making the correct speech sounds – this can be to do with confusion about the system of sounds, or a physical difficulty in saying them. Remember that a child who has English as an additional language may well be slow to speak in English in your setting, but this does not necessarily mean that the child has a language delay. Be aware of the signs of potential communication difficulties. For instance, if the child:

- ✓ Does not respond to sounds as you would expect;
- ✓ Seems to have problems understanding requests or instructions;
- ✓ Often appears to have difficulty paying attention to what practitioners are saying;

- ✓ Speaks in a way that seems unusual, compared to others of the same age;
- ✓ Talks particularly slowly, or makes a number of mistakes with pronunciation;
- ✓ Struggles to make friends or to join in with other children's games;
- ✓ For older children, cannot seem to pick up the initial sound of a word;
- ✓ Does not seem to be learning and developing in the way you would normally expect for his or her age.

To support children who have language and/or communication difficulties:

- ✓ Make sure that you have a system in place to track children's communication skills, and to identify children who might be experiencing difficulties. Be aware of the expected progress of language development for different age groups.
- ✓ Where you have concerns, speak to parents and aim to get specialist input as quickly as possible. It is important to intervene rapidly when small children have any kind of language delay.
- ✓ Bear the children's chronological ages and emotional confidence in mind when assessing for language delay or difficulty.
- ✓ Where you identify a problem, look for specialist support from speech and language therapists and work alongside parents to allay any concerns. This is a complex area, and children with difficulties need specialist input.

The Fourth V:

Visual and Non-Verbal Communication

The Fourth V: Visual and Non-Verbal Communication

As well as using talk to communicate, we can also use a variety of visual and non-verbal methods to 'speak' to our children. Visual approaches help children grasp meaning before they can read. Small children very quickly learn to 'read' symbols, such as a brand of a fast food outlet or a tick for yes/well done. Visual communication can also help parents with different home languages to access your setting, and to feel welcomed and supported.

Visual Communication

It is very important to use visual communication with young children, because they do not yet have the reading skills required to deal with written language. When using visual communication, take care that the walls and other surfaces in your setting do not become excessively busy. This can make it harder for children to see what is there, and to understand the visual or symbolic messages you are giving. To develop visual communication in your setting:

- ✓ Allocate a picture to each of your children, one that starts with the same letter as their name, and preferably one that links to their interests. For instance, you might have a train picture for Teri or a ball picture for Bethany. Wherever you use the children's names (on coat pegs, book trays, etc.) use the image alongside the name, to help them link the two.
- ✓ For drawers of resources, add photos of what is inside. As an interesting alternative, stick the actual resource onto the outside of the drawer (eg. a Lego brick or a pencil).

- ✓ Have a visual method for registration – in our setting we get the children to stick up their name labels to say whether they want milk or water to drink at snack time (with parents' help as needed). You could use a register on your interactive whiteboard, asking the children to put their name under a smiley or a sad face, depending on how they are feeling that day.
- ✓ In places where you need to give instructions – for instance, 'how to wash your hands' in the bathroom – put up a series of pictures to show the steps that the children should take.
- ✓ Use visual timetables for small children, and particularly for those children with English as an additional language, or those with learning difficulties.
- ✓ An 'emotions board' is a lovely way to encourage children to think and talk about their feelings. Stick up pictures of people showing different emotions, or some simple emoticons, to discuss with your children.
- ✓ Colours can be very useful to communicate meaning – from a young age we learn to associate red with stop/danger. However, be aware that around 1 in 12 children (mainly boys) will have a deficit in seeing colours. Be aware that this may not be picked up until they are much older, as the check for colour deficit is no longer a statutory part of the NHS eye test.
- ✓ With reception age children, use visual methods to assess and give feedback on their written work. You can use different colours to indicate different aspects of a piece of writing – for instance using pink to highlight an excellent idea, or green to indicate targets for the future.
- ✓ Display samples of children's learning, such as artwork, or pieces of mark making or writing, as a visual way to celebrate their achievements.

- ✓ Display samples of writing from other languages, and images of people from different cultural backgrounds, as a visual reminder of the rich diversity of different cultures.
- ✓ Have a board with photos of your key workers on it, and stick the children's photographs around each one, to remind parents who their child's key worker is.
- ✓ Use images to indicate different areas of your setting, for instance a picture of pencils and paper for your writing area.
- ✓ Use visual methods for rewards, such as stickers and stars. Give WOW slips to parents, so they can note down the great things that their children do at home, and send these in to communicate the child's achievements with the setting.
- ✓ Use visual approaches to help you manage behaviour, for instance having a set of 'Golden Rules' with pictures to help the children understand what they mean. Staff should model appropriate behaviour for the children, to show them what it looks like.

Non-Verbal Communication

For babies and very young children, verbal communication is difficult. At first, they can only pick out a few words from the sounds that surround them, and they can only use a few sounds in return. Help your children gather meaning from what you say by giving them lots of non-verbal signals to help them understand what is going on. Non-verbal communication is typically very subtle, but children naturally use it to help them construct meaning from what is being said. The types of non-verbal communication you use will include:

- ✓ **Eye contact and eye movements:** Eye contact tells a child that we are interested in what he or she is saying. You can widen your eyes to show interest and to gain a child's attention. Narrowing your eyes helps show that you are curious about something.
- ✓ **Facial expressions:** Our faces are amazingly helpful in communicating the meaning of what we are saying. You can purse your lips and widen your eyes to show that you are saying something surprising, or scrunch up your forehead to show that you are puzzled.
- ✓ **Hand gestures:** Our hands are one of the most expressive parts of our bodies. We can use hand gestures in a huge variety of ways. We can show where something is within space, for instance indicating 'high up' with a hand above our heads, or 'come here' by beckoning. We can gesture to show emotion, for example holding our hands up, palms flat, to show surprise.
- ✓ **Body language and posture:** When we want to 'read' what someone is thinking or feeling, we will look at the person's body as well. An upright posture indicates confidence, while hands on hips can indicate irritation or aggression.
- ✓ **Use of space:** When we move in close to the children, it shows that we are interested, and want to make a connection with them. Sitting or crouching down, to make sure you are at the children's level, is very important for effective communication.

Non-verbal communication is very much a two-way street. As well as teachers and practitioners thinking carefully about the non-verbal messages they send, we also need to be very sensitive to the non-verbal messages that our children give us as well. The way that a child stands, or moves around your setting, will tell you a great deal about his or her emotional or psychological state. When you do observations, as well as thinking about the child's learning, consider what his or her non-verbal signals or gestures tell you about how he or she is feeling.

Non-verbal approaches will also help you manage behaviour. The great thing about non-verbal signals is that they keep the issue private, and reduce the likelihood of confrontation. For instance, you might catch a child's eye to show that you have spotted what is going on, or use a hand signal to indicate that you want the child to calm down or move away.

Alternative Methods of Communication

Many settings now use signing systems such as Makaton to support children's communication and understanding. These systems are very useful to teach and use, even if none of the current children at your setting have specific language or communication difficulties. Children take naturally to the use of non-verbal signs and signals – they find this way of communicating instinctive and perfectly normal. You can incorporate signs in many ways – when talking to individual children, when singing together, when giving instructions, and so on.

The Communication Trust offers a very helpful booklet entitled 'Other Ways of Speaking', which gives advice and information on augmentative and alternative communication for children with learning difficulties or disabilities: www.thecommunicationtrust.org.uk/media/3414/other_ways_of_speaking_final.pdf.

The Fifth V:

Variety

The Fifth V: Variety

A great early years setting offers the children access to a variety of resources, environments, experiences and approaches, to help them learn new skills, to develop their thinking, and to learn more about their world. The wider the range of possibilities you offer, the richer the experience will be for your children. This is particularly so for those children who do not get the chance to encounter this variety outside your setting. Children benefit hugely from being immersed in different experiences, and interacting with a variety of objects and environments. The more multi-sensory and diverse experiences children have when they are young, the more they develop a rich base of language and knowledge to build upon as they grow older.

A Variety of Skills and Subjects

Young children are like sponges – they constantly soak up information from the people and the world around them. In the early years, children tend to learn skills and subjects in an interconnected way. A child building a tower of blocks with a practitioner could be learning colours, how to count, concepts around balance and forces, fine motor skills, and so on. In order to learn more about different subjects, children need the adults to offer the right kind of resources and information as they play. In order to learn new skills, children need the adults to model techniques (for instance, tying a knot or using scissors) and to get the opportunity for lots and lots of practice.

Find a method for planning to ensure you are covering the different subjects and skills within the EYFS framework. At our setting we use a large (A3) size 'Continuous Provision' planning sheet, with boxes for each area of our provision – role play, sand/water, small world, reading area, outdoors, and so on. We make a note in each box explaining the resources that are on offer that day, and the areas of learning that these cover. We also note whether an activity is child or adult initiated, or adult directed. During the day staff add notes about next steps for individual children to this sheet, and identify any specific interests or needs that have been observed during the session. Our planning is very much a working document, with staff adding to it as they work, rather than a 'lesson' planned ahead of time. It gives us an easily accessible overview of our provision, and also a useful record of what individual children have been doing during each week.

Find a method of assessment to ensure that all children develop in all the areas of learning. It is useful to have an overview of the areas of learning in the children's learning journeys or profiles, so that you can highlight the different subjects and skills as you cover them. Have a separate detailed assessment for each child's speech and language development (we use a very good format provided by our local authority). Link staff training to all the areas of learning, and use your self-evaluation process to identify where staff need to develop their skills. Share staff expertise around, so that where one staff member has an interest or skill in a particular area, they get a chance to share their ideas and techniques with others.

A Variety of Resources

One of the most important things we can offer our children is high quality, interesting and multi-sensory resources with which to play and learn. This is not about buying-in the latest technology or the shiniest toys – children are often just as fascinated by the box that the toy comes in, as the toy itself. Variety of resources is about a creative use of resources and materials, and about thinking ahead when you invest in new ones. Ideally, look for resources that are:

- ✓ Multi-sensory, so that they inspire the children to touch, taste, smell, look and listen. Often, the best multi-sensory resources are those from the natural world – plants and natural materials such as bark, pine cones, sand, clay, and so on.
- ✓ Easy to access, so that the children can get 'hands-on' with them easily. Safe, accessible storage is a key issue for early years settings to consider.
- ✓ Multi-purpose, so that they can be used for various activities or subject areas, and so that they work for the different age groups in your setting.
- ✓ Easy to clean, good value, high quality and long lasting. Resources need to be safe, difficult to damage, and sustainable for the longer term.
- ✓ Safe for the spread of ages within your setting. If you have very young children in a space with older ones, you will need to manage choking hazards very carefully.

Remember that your staff members, and the time that they spend with the children, are the most valuable resource you have in your setting. At our setting we choose to invest in a high ratio of staff to children, and as much training and time for discussion as we can afford, rather than expensive toys and equipment.

Finding Great Resources

The best resources are often those that you find by accident, that are recycled from something else, or that are used in a different way to that which was intended. Often, one resource will become something else over time, because of the way that the children show you they want to use it. For instance, a planted area in our garden close to the tap has now been given over to a mud kitchen, in response to the way that the children were playing with it. To give you inspiration, here are some creative ways we have used resources in our setting:

- ✓ **The giant spaceship box:** We bought a giant, wardrobe-sized box from a well-known storage company. The children decided it should become a spaceship, which was achieved with the addition of portholes and plenty of silver foil. Later on, the box was recycled to form part of a Christmas display. A pile of empty boxes is a great resource for 'deconstructed role play', with the children deciding what they want the boxes to become.
- ✓ **The magic climbing frame:** We have an indoor climbing frame that has been turned into many different things over the years. One time it was a Princess Castle; another time it was a Superhero Den. Sometimes it even gets used as a climbing frame.
- ✓ **The multi-purpose tarpaulin:** We sit on our tarpaulin when the ground is wet, and we hang it up to create a den or a sunshade when it is sunny. We also use it as a windbreak when we are out and about, for instance at a very windy primary school sports day.
- ✓ **The multi-use net curtain wire:** In our packaway setting, we use lengths of net curtain wire to hang displays around the room, so that they are easy to put up and take down. We have also used wire threaded with

gauze and colourful scarves, to create a quiet reading area in one corner of the room.

Managing Resources

As well as getting hold of great resources, you also need to manage them and plan for their use and re-use. This can be a time consuming part of the job. There are lots of great resources on offer, and it's tempting to buy in lots of new toys or games, rather than thinking about how you might re-use your old ones. Here are some general tips for managing your resources to get the very best out of them:

- ✓ **Keep them tidy:** A resource is only useful if it can be easily accessed. If it is hidden in a dusty cupboard, or under a pile of other less useful resources, then it is effectively worthless. Looking after and organising resources takes time, but it is time well spent, particularly when you want children to be able to access them easily. Whatever the type of storage system you use – moveable or fixed shelving units, cupboards, clear plastic boxes, and so on – set aside time to keep them tidy and well organised.
- ✓ **Keep children's access in mind:** We store our resources in clear plastic boxes, so that children and staff can see at a glance what is in them. Boxes are labelled with a photograph of what is inside. We had shelves built that were just the right width and depth for boxes to be lined up side by side, so that each box can be seen at a glance. Where you have fixed storage, ensure that this is at the children's height and not the adults'.
- ✓ **Edit them regularly:** Less is definitely more when it comes to resources. There are many great resources out there and you need to be strong-willed not to let your

setting get full of stuff. The problem with having too many resources is that the best ones get forgotten or become impossible to access. Set aside a time each year when you will audit the resources you have – we do an annual sort out over the Summer holidays. You could sell your spare resources to parents, or on an auction website, to raise funds.

- ✓ **Keep a regularly updated list:** Create a list of all the resources in your setting, divided into different age groups as appropriate. Make sure your list is accessible to all staff, so that they can use it when planning for activities and for next steps. For instance, you could hang a copy on the inside of a storage cupboard, or on the wall of your setting.
- ✓ **Involve the children:** Encourage the children to learn how to take care of resources, with 'tidying away together' a part of your daily routine. Ask the children which resources they enjoy playing with, especially when planning to invest in something new.
- ✓ **Recycle and reuse:** Learn to see any object as a potential resource. When those crisps that come in tubes have been eaten, the tubes provide a great source of inspiration – you can make telescopes, kaleidoscopes, shakers, and so on. If you are lucky enough to have a local Scrapstore (www.scrapstoresuk.org) these offer a great source of recycled materials for the early years.

Creating your Own Resources

You can make some wonderful resources of your own, by thinking creatively about what to use, and how to use it. For a great source of inspiration, take a look at 'Tishylishy's'

Pinterest page (www.uk.pinterest.com/tishylishy/). Here are some ideas you might like to try:

- ✓ Paint letters and graphemes on pebbles, to turn them into a literacy aid.
- ✓ Write letters and graphemes onto lollypop sticks, for the children to practise identifying letters or making words.
- ✓ Write letters or numbers/symbols onto polystyrene cups, then fix them together so that the children can turn them to create different words or sums.
- ✓ Put a cable reel on its side, to use as a table.
- ✓ Fix a variety of locks and bolts to a wooden board, so that the children can turn them to build fine motor skills.
- ✓ Paint the children's names onto rocks, put them into a basket, and challenge them to 'find their name', or use these for registration.
- ✓ Recycle small bowls by putting beads and other small items into them, giving the children chopsticks to practise their fine motor skills by picking them up.
- ✓ Create a sewing table, by attaching material to a wooden frame and fixing it on top of the table.

A Variety of Environments/Experiences

Although the home is important in the early years, and offers a place of safety and security, children also need access to a variety of environments and a range of enriching experiences. This supports their early learning and development, and also helps them to cope with difference and change. Young children might play at a friend's house, spend time kicking a ball or swinging and sliding in the park, visit a museum, and spend a day on the beach. This variety helps children to:

- ✓ Develop their vocabulary as they hear talk used in different ways and places;
- ✓ Learn how people use language in different settings and situations;
- ✓ Build their knowledge about the world, and the people within it;
- ✓ Learn to manage risk, for instance in outdoor environments;
- ✓ Explore their world, and become more independent within it;
- ✓ Understand different perspectives and viewpoints;
- ✓ Develop their sense of empathy and learn how to play co-operatively.

Make sure that you take your children out of your setting, and into different environments, as often as you can. You can find lots more ideas about doing this in the next section.

The Setting Environment

As well as taking the children on trips and visits, you can also offer a variety of environments and experiences within your setting. This will happen both through the resources and equipment you have on offer, and also through the way that you organise your setting. Consider the following aspects of your provision:

- ✓ **Freeflow:** Ideally, children should be able to move freely between the indoor and the outdoor environments in your setting, so that they have as much choice as possible about where and how to play. It might be that staffing, space or safety constraints mean that this is only possible for some of the time children are in your setting. If this is the case for you, designate a time for outdoor play or hold a 'forest school' session once or twice a week. With a bit of lateral thinking, it is often possible to create freeflow between indoors and outdoors in the most unlikely of spaces. Our building opens onto a tarmac parking area and at first it seemed as though it would be impossible for us to offer freeflow. However, we purchased some metal barriers to make a partition, and created a small garden on a thin strip of wasteland alongside the building, to allow us to use the freeflow approach.

✓ **Private spaces:** Include some quiet areas, so that the children have a place to go when they want to focus on a book or simply sit and be calm. This is especially important if you have younger children in your setting – for instance, if you are planning to extend nursery class provision to 2 year olds. If your setting is one open space (as ours is), then use curtains, soft furnishings or partitions to mark out a quiet area separate from the main space. Incorporate somewhere soft and comfy to sit, such as a sofa or bean bags, so that children can spend as much time here as they wish. You might set up a book corner or, if you have the space, you could designate an entire room within your setting as a place for quiet activities.

✓ **Displays:** It is tempting to believe that, with displays, it is 'the more the merrier'. However, take care that the walls of your setting do not become over cluttered, as this makes it hard for the children to focus on what is there. Ensure that displays are at child height, rather than at adult height. Try not to use too much colour or detail in any one part of your room. A two or three coloured display works well – black and white, or primary colours. Remember to include other community languages on displays. You can also incorporate multi-sensory aspects, such as different textures, or recordable 'talk buttons' for sound. A 'Cabinet of Curiosities' display is a great place for small 'discovered' items that children so love to collect, such as pretty shells or pebbles from a beach, or an old bird's nest.

✓ **Lighting:** Consider how you make use of both natural and artificial light in your setting. Create dark, quiet spaces using tents, large boxes and torches. Use spotlights to highlight particular areas in a room, and a lightbox for displaying interesting items. Consider how you can use the light that comes through the windows to highlight children's artwork, for instance by making 'stained glass' effect pictures with coloured cellophane.

Variety in the Outdoor Environment

The outside area at your setting offers a great place for a variety of learning experiences, and is particularly appropriate for messy activities. To make the most of your outdoor area:

✓ Grow plants from seed with your children – sunflowers are great for measuring activities, and crops such as carrots are easy and very rewarding to grow.
✓ Join the RHS Gardens for Schools scheme, which offers support and funding to help schools and preschools do more gardening with their children.
✓ Use the ground for a variety of purposes – creating a 'doormat' with coloured chalks, or drawing 'roads' on which to drive ride-on toys.
✓ If you have trees growing in your outdoor area, use these to build dens, to do bark rubbing, or to do measuring activities.

- ✓ Encourage your children to listen for sounds in the outdoors – for instance, helping them learn to identify different bird songs.
- ✓ A pond is a fantastic resource for learning more about nature and wildlife. For safety purposes, we bought a specialist grid to cover our pond.

Think laterally when considering the areas of learning that can be covered in the outdoor part of your setting. Bring literacy into the outdoors, by using outdoor surfaces to make marks. Have a 'literacy kit' to take with you when you go outside, with clipboards, pencils and other mark making equipment. Consider all the ways that children can develop their numeracy outside – for instance, measuring distances, counting the steps they take, using timers, and playing hopscotch.

A Variety of Approaches

The Foundation Stage runs from birth right through to the age of five, and a single approach is never going to be suitable for all the different age groups. As practitioners know, working in the early years is about balance, variety and finding the right approach for each individual child. Look to achieve the appropriate balance between adult directed learning, adult initiated activities, and child initiated learning/play, depending on the age and needs of your children. As well as letting your young children feel free to play, use your knowledge about early child development to help them learn as effectively as possible. The balance you use will depend on the specific needs of your children, their age, and your context. The balance of approaches will change as the children get older, and during the course of the academic year. There are three main approaches to learning used in early years settings:

- ✓ **Adult directed learning:** The adult sets up an activity and directs the children to participate in it, or to complete it. This approach works well for activities where the children learn to follow a series of instructions, for instance sports, or preparing snacks. It also works well for teaching specific skills, such as phonics or letter formation, particularly in a reception class. When you want or need a child to move on to a specific 'next step', you might use an adult directed task or activity to teach that next step. For older children, being able to follow adult instructions is part of the 'step-up' in preparation for the more formal atmosphere of Key Stage One. Sometimes, adult-directed learning is done with a whole group – for instance, when playing parachute games. At other times, you might direct an activity for a smaller group, perhaps the older children in a mixed age setting.
- ✓ **Adult initiated learning:** This type of learning is initiated or inspired by the adult, but there is no compulsion for the children to get involved, or to complete a specific task. Often, these activities are set up in response to something that the practitioners have observed about a child. For instance, where the children are showing a keen interest in 'superheroes', the adult might initiate a role play by setting up a 'superhero headquarters' and encouraging the children to come into the setting dressed up in costumes.
- ✓ **Child initiated learning:** In this situation the child is left to decide what kind of play he or she would like to do. The adult might get involved and play alongside the

child, using sustained shared thinking, or leave the child to play independently or with his or her peers. In child initiated learning, the adult typically follows the child's directions, while at the same time incorporating learning opportunities (for instance, helping children learn to count blocks as they build a tower).

Variety: Valuing Diversity

Ensure that your setting values difference and diversity in its widest sense, by celebrating and acknowledging the way that different people live their lives. Do an audit of the resources you have in your setting, to ensure that they are diverse and representative of different backgrounds and cultures. Take your children on visits to different places, and invite visitors from the community into your setting.

Think ahead about the diverse needs of the local children, and where possible make adaptations ahead of time, before a child arrives in your setting. For instance, you might ask your local authority for help with physical adaptations to the setting, to support a child with a disability who will be attending your setting in the future. Liase with specialists in your local authority team about the best way to meet the language, access and support needs of different members of your community.

The Sixth V:

Visits, Visitors and Volunteers

The Sixth V: Visits, Visitors and Volunteers

Visits, visitors and volunteers play a key part in your mission to give the children access to a range of environments and experiences, and to create a 'family' feeling at your setting. You might take the children on a trip to somewhere that they could not otherwise visit – the zoo, the theatre, a museum, a steam train ride, a forest, a city farm. You can also create different environments *within* your setting – a fairytale castle, a veterinary surgery, a grocery shop. Visits and visitors really enrich the learning that your children do while they are with you. Parents are always delighted to know that their children have had the chance to experience something new.

Trips and Visits

Although there are logistical issues involved, trips and visits do not have to be complicated or expensive. At our setting we arrange a regular end of year Summer trip for the children and their families, but we also go on various local trips over the course of the year. You might:

- ✓ Take your children on walks to local areas of interest – perhaps a park or a nature reserve. We are lucky enough to have a stone circle that we can visit near our setting.
- ✓ Arrange visits to your local primary schools, to support transition, in conjunction with local teachers.
- ✓ Organise a weekly outdoor session, to a local forest or wild area if you have one, or just to go for a walk.
- ✓ Approach your local old people's home, to ask whether you can bring your children in to visit, perhaps to sing some songs.

✓ Arrange to visit local places of worship, to help the children learn more about different religious beliefs.

Before you go on any trips or visits, do a full risk assessment and think ahead about the equipment that you will need to take with you, including a first aid kit. At our setting, we purchased a small, wheeled cart that we use to transport equipment when we do forest school or gardening sessions. Before you go, talk with the children about safe and appropriate behaviour in the place you will be visiting. Get as many staff, parents or volunteers along to help you out as you can, to help you keep the children safe outside the setting.

Visits and Transition

Eventually, children who are at a private or voluntary run early years setting will move on to the reception class at a primary school. Before your children transfer to school, think ahead about the process of transition, and how you can support your children in the move. Visits, and visitors, are a great way to form links with your local primary schools. For instance, in our setting, we:

✓ Host regular visits from the children at our local primary school. The previous year's reception children visit our setting to share their oral story telling, as part of Pie Corbett's 'Story Making Project' that is used both at our preschool and at the local primary school.
✓ Find ways to link the curriculum between your early years setting and the primary school. For instance, our children are already well acquainted with the techniques used in the 'Story Making Project' when they encounter them in their reception class.

- ✓ Make a Transition Booklet for your children to take into school, with sections for them to draw their new classroom, a picture of their new teacher, and so on.
- ✓ Arrange to attend various school productions at local primaries during the year – from the Christmas Nativity play to the Summer show.
- ✓ Liase with your local primary schools so that your children can take part in school events during the year, such as an annual sports day.
- ✓ Publicise events held by your local schools, to your parents, such as school fairs or a Halloween party.
- ✓ Consider how you can liase with all phases of local education, for instance by linking up with local secondary schools to offer work placements, or with a local college that runs a childcare course.

Visitors

Encourage lots of visitors to come into your setting, including all the different members of your children's families and your local community, and also by arranging specialist paid for events. By making your setting feel open and welcoming, you will help people see it as a key part of their local community. You will also help the children learn more about difference and diversity. Ensure that you:

- ✓ Find ways to involve siblings, grandparents, and other members of the extended family in your setting. This might be through setting up fun events for the whole family, or by creating opportunities to visit and see what you do – for instance on an open day, or at a workshop for parents.
- ✓ Encourage mums, dads and other carers to get involved, where possible. This might be a 'one off' (e.g. hosting a

'Dads Read with Kids' Day at your setting) but it can also be part of your ongoing mission. Many grandparents are keen to get involved, and have time to spare. They are often happy to come in to read with the children, or share a skill, so be sure to ask.

✓ Invite people from the local community into your setting, for instance local religious leaders, fire fighters, or police community support officers, so that you can all learn more about and from each other.

There are many specialist organisations that will visit your setting. There is often a charge, so you might need to fundraise or ask parents for a voluntary contribution to cover the costs. Over the years we have invited various specialist groups into our setting. For example:

✓ **Rainforest Adventure:** A team of specialists came into our setting to show the children different kinds of rainforest creatures. The experience was enriched by the use of costumes and storytelling, and the children were able to handle some of the creatures.
✓ **Birds of Prey:** A local birds of prey group visited our setting with various different birds. The children learned more about owls and other large birds, and those who wanted to could handle some of the birds.
✓ **Yoga:** A local yoga teacher visited our setting over the course of several terms, using children's stories, such as *The Very Hungry Caterpillar*, to teach yoga moves to the children.

Volunteers

As a voluntary run preschool, our setting relies on a team of volunteers to form our management committee, as well as on a team of fundraising volunteers to bring in additional funds. Most of our volunteers are parents of our children, but we also have helpers who do not have children at our setting (other local people, grandparents, and so on). Even if your setting is not voluntary run, volunteers can still play a vital role in making your provision as great as it can possibly be. When working with young children, the more adults who are available to help, the better. A volunteer can offer one to one support for children, for instance to help with reading, or specialist expertise, for instance in IT. To encourage people to volunteer at your setting:

- ✓ Make sure that you ask! It is often the case that people would be happy to help, but no one asks them, or explains what they can do. Practitioners often have a fair idea of which parents or family members would be most likely to help, and can approach individuals to ask.
- ✓ Be clear about the job that you need or want your volunteers to do. We have a job description for different committee roles, and a document to explain the process for volunteers to join our team (including how to complete DBS checks and fill in Ofsted forms).
- ✓ Suggest ways that volunteers could help you, but allow people to bring their own skills into play. For instance, a parent who is a musician might offer to do some music sessions in your setting.
- ✓ Ask around within your local community, as well as within your setting. Church groups will often be keen to support other local community enterprises.
- ✓ Don't give up at the first hurdle, if your requests for volunteers are not met immediately. We often find that we have to ask several times, before people decide to volunteer.

The Seventh V:

Viability

The Seventh V: Viability

You can create the best early years setting in the world, but if it is not able to operate within its means, it will not be able to stay open. For an early years setting to survive long term, it needs to work as a viable and sustainable model. There is an incredibly diverse range of types of provision within the early years sector. From privately run nurseries, some of which are part of a chain, to state run nursery classes in infant and primary schools, to childminders who set up in business by themselves, to the voluntary run part of the sector, where settings are often also constituted as charities.

Whatever kind of setting you run or work within, it is crucial to protect the long-term viability of your setting. You must make sure you set and stick to budgets, buy quality resources that are value for money, ensure that there is sufficient demand for the service you offer, and market your setting to local families. You may also need to apply for charitable grants, organise fundraising, and find other sources of revenue to keep afloat. This section covers the key areas that you need to consider.

Financial Management

When I started working as part of the management team at our preschool, I knew very little about financial management. Several years later, I know an awful lot more and I can read and understand our cashflow and accounts. However, I also know enough to appreciate that dealing with finances is a specialised job that needs to be done by people with expertise. To ensure your long-term viability, you need:

- ✓ An accountant or finance manager to oversee your finances, prepare cashflows and budgets, and someone fully qualified to prepare your annual accounts. Depending on the type of setting, your accounts may need to be independently audited as well.
- ✓ A treasurer who will manage your money day to day, handling cash and authorising payments into and out of your bank account.
- ✓ Someone to calculate and prepare invoices, and to submit paperwork to your local authority so that you receive the correct funding.
- ✓ Budgets for spending in all areas, set annually but reviewed monthly. You must budget for wages, employer's national insurance, payroll, Ofsted fees, insurance, resources, rent, rates, utilities, professional services, staff uniform, maintenance of equipment, accounting, food for snacks, trips, visitors, and so on.
- ✓ Methods to ensure that staff stick to budgets, keep a record of the money that they spend, and get 'sign-off' for more expensive purchases.
- ✓ A cashflow that shows how much cash you have in the bank at any one time, so that you are sure you can pay staff salaries and other costs over the course of the year.
- ✓ A reserve fund to cover wages, redundancy payments, and other costs, should your setting have to close. Any spare funds will help you stay afloat during quiet years, or help you cover the cost of expanding your setting.
- ✓ To keep a handle on staffing costs, as these are the main expenditure for any setting. Overtime, in particular, can have a negative impact on your overall annual spending.
- ✓ To ensure that you comply with the appropriate regulations governing your finances. For instance if your setting is constituted as a charity, you will need to

prepare accounts, have them audited, and then submit them before the annual deadline to the Charities Commission.
- ✓ To think and plan ahead, about how changes to childcare funding or provision may affect your setting. For example, at the moment we are talking about how we will manage to implement the government's new offer of 30 hours 'free' childcare for working parents.

Once you have your cashflow in place, find a regular time to sit down and work through it, line by line, looking at how current income and spending matches up to projected income and expenditure. Identify all future spending and income, and ensure that it is all recorded in your cashflow. Check that staff are sticking to budgets, and that any unexpected costs, such as overtime, are kept in check. It is best to over estimate spending, and under estimate expenditure, rather than the other way around. Remember that, in a small setting, one or two additional children can make a big difference to your income.

At our preschool we use various people to do the different finance jobs: a volunteer committee member works as treasurer to handle cash and make payments, an administrative assistant keeps a record of spending and income, and a qualified accountant manages the cashflow and draws up our accounts. One of the key issues with managing costs in an early years setting is that the children do not necessarily arrive in one neat group, as they do in school. You may find, like us, that September is a quiet time, because the older children have moved on to school and the younger ones are not yet attending full time. In our setting, numbers gradually increase over the course of the academic year, with a large part of our income coming in the Summer term.

Remember that staffing is your main cost, and this will vary according to the salaries you pay, the ratios you use, the level of qualifications your staff have, and so on. The way that you staff your setting is closely linked to the vision discussed in the first section of this book. At our setting, we place a priority on a high ratio of highly qualified staff to children. Even though we have a graduate leader and could use a ratio of 1 adult to 13 children, we fundraise to maintain a ratio of at least 1 adult to every 5 children.

Marketing

Marketing your setting is about ensuring that you are visible to local parents, so that they know who you are, where you are, and what kind of provision you offer. Positive word of mouth is probably the most powerful kind of marketing that you have available. Parents tend to trust what other parents and local people say, when finding the most appropriate early years setting for their own children. To market your setting:

- ✓ Ensure that you appear on the local authority list of childcare in your area, and in any other childcare lists available locally.
- ✓ Have a banner or sign in a prominent place outside your setting.
- ✓ Make flyers to have available at local events, and ask whether you can display them in local shops and on outdoor noticeboards.
- ✓ Use paid advertising and editorial content in local newspapers to market your setting. When anything newsworthy happens at your setting, email information

and photographs to the editor. Invite a press contact to key events and (politely) chase them up to ensure that your story gets featured.
- ✓ Place adverts in any free press that is distributed to families in your area, including parish magazines in rural areas.
- ✓ Use your website as a starting point for your online marketing, keeping it up to date and making sure that it looks attractive to prospective parents. Consider setting up a Facebook and Twitter account for your setting, although be aware that this needs careful management and will take up staff time.
- ✓ Ask parents who use your setting about how they first heard about you. This can really help you to refine your marketing strategy.
- ✓ Create a 'logo' for your setting, to use on banners, uniforms, your website, and so on.
- ✓ Host regular open days to invite new families to visit your setting, to see how it is run, and what you can offer their children.
- ✓ Encourage current parents to recommend your setting to their friends.
- ✓ If you have contacts in local toddler groups, pay them a visit to highlight what your setting has to offer.

Fundraising

Many early years settings will do some form of fundraising, to raise additional funds to cover their costs, and to buy in 'extras' such as trips or equipment for the children. This is particularly the case for school-based and voluntary run settings, which often rely mainly on government funding rather than on fees. If your setting is a charity, you will be eligible to apply for various charitable grants as well. To boost your fundraising efforts:

- ✓ Run events that combine fun with fundraising, for instance parties, family fun days, and special pamper nights for parents.
- ✓ Ask around about grants that are available from local groups and trusts. Keep an eye out for adverts about these in your local paper.
- ✓ Some banks and other businesses run a 'match funding' scheme, where they match any funds that staff fundraise for charity. Ask your parents to check whether they work for an organisation that offers this scheme.
- ✓ The lottery 'Awards for All' scheme is a good source of funding for special events, although be aware that the application process is time consuming.
- ✓ Your local authority may offer grants for specific purposes, for instance we applied for and received a grant to help us develop our outdoor area.

Printed in Great Britain
by Amazon